EXTRAORDINARY ORDINARY PEOPLE

FIVE AMERICAN MASTERS OF TRADITIONAL ARTS

ALAN GOVENAR

CANDLEWICK PRESS
CAMBRIDGE, MASSACHUSETTS

First edition 2006

Library of Congress Cataloging-in-Publication Data

Govenar, Alan B., date.
Extraordinary ordinary people : five American masters of traditional arts /
Alan Govenar. — 1st ed.
p.   cm.
Includes bibliographical references.
ISBN 0-7636-2047-5
1. Folk art — United States.
2. Folk artists — United States — Biography.
3. Handicraft — United States.
I. Title.
NK808.G68 2006
745.092'273 — dc22   2005044864

2 4 6 8 10 9 7 5 3 1

Printed in Singapore

This book was typeset in Berling.

Candlewick Press
2067 Massachusetts Avenue
Cambridge, Massachusetts 02140

visit us at www.candlewick.com

To the memory of my father,
Joseph Govenar
1921–2004

CONTENTS

INTRODUCTION

. . . .

For as long as I can remember, I have preferred back roads to freeways, subways to taxis, walking to driving. I savor the sense of place, the colors of house paint and trim, the styles of clothing, makeup, and hair, the tastes, the landscapes, the sidewalks, the sounds, the smells, the music, the people I meet, the feeling of being inside the world as life happens. In my travels, I have learned that the varied texture of American life has been shaped by the people who have lived here for centuries, and by those who have migrated here by choice or necessity. Each region of this vast nation has its own character, elaborated by its geography and by its astonishing mix of cultures.

Extraordinary Ordinary People is a journey across America through the lives and creativity of five individuals. They are ordinary to the extent they may remind us of people we know in our families or among our neighbors and friends. They may be unrecognizable outside the communities where they live and work, but they are extraordinary in their passion and commitment to artistic excellence. They are innovators and teachers, eager to share their skills and knowledge.

Each is a recipient of the National Heritage Fellowship, presented annually since 1982 by the National Endowment for the Arts to recognize the ongoing ingenuity of individuals who have mastered different culturally defined art forms. They live in every region of America—whether in inner-city neighborhoods, in sprawling suburbs, or along country roads. They are dedicated to time-honored traditions that are often passed on from one generation to the next by word of mouth and customary example.

Qi Shu Fang is a *wu-dan*, a Beijing Opera singer, who, after touring worldwide, left China in 1988 at the height of her career. With her husband, Ding Mei-Kui, she founded the Qi Shu Fang Peking Opera Company in New York City to preserve and nurture Beijing Opera in the United States.* Most of the members of her company are Chinese immigrants, many of whom work at unrelated day jobs in restaurants or the garment industry but are nonetheless committed to Beijing Opera as a means of perpetuating their culture and history.

Ralph W. Stanley grew up in Southwest Harbor, Maine, on Mount Desert Island. As a boy, he liked to watch the boat builders whose shops were scattered along the waterfront. In the late 1940s, he decided he wanted his own boat but couldn't afford to buy one, and over the next two years he built himself a lobster boat. A few months after he finished, someone asked him to build another, and he's built about one or two a year since then.

In Nyssa, Oregon, not far from the Montana border, Genoveva "Eva" Castellanoz fashions *coronas*—crowns handmade from tiny

---

* *Peking* and *Beijing* are two names for one place, the capital city of the People's Republic of China. *Peking* is the old Western spelling. *Beijing* is the spelling in pinyin, a phonetic system that the Chinese government has favored since the 1960s.

pieces of twisted paper, which are then dipped in wax and shaped into *azahares*, or orange buds, a Mexican symbol of purity. One *corona* takes countless hours to make and may have as many as one thousand *azahares*. *Coronas* are often worn by fifteen-year-old girls coming of age at their *quinceañeras* or by brides on their wedding days.

Dorothy Trumpold is a weaver who grew up in the Amana Colonies, a communal society in Iowa founded by German immigrants in the mid-nineteenth century. As a child, she loved to watch her grandfather weave, and in 1940, when his health began to fail, she taught herself to weave on his loom. In time, she mastered the craft of making rag rugs, using scraps of cotton and wool to create wall-to-wall carpets in her home and the homes of people in her community.

Allison "Tootie" Montana made his living as a lather, fabricating the framework for domes, arches, and other building forms, but spent his free time for more than fifty years creating Mardi Gras Indian "suits"—elegantly sewn and beaded regalia, each of which takes a year to make and a day to debut in the Creole and African American neighborhood where he lived in New Orleans.*

The stories of these incredible people are told mostly through their own words, edited from my interviews with each of them over the years. The stories they tell speak to the importance of determination, perseverance, and humor. Once you meet each of these five individuals and their art forms, you are likely to remember them and, perhaps, become more aware of your own world and the people who embody the creative spirit among us.

*Allison "Tootie" Montana died on June 27, 2005, as this book was going to press.

Qi Shu Fang

Beijing Opera Performer

Overleaf: Qi Shu Fang as Mu Gui Ying, the wu-dan *role in* Women Generals of the Yang Family.

Right: Backstage at the Kaye Playhouse in midtown Manhattan, the cast and crew make preparations for the Peking (Beijing) Opera Company production of Women Generals of the Yang Family, *2002.*

QI SHU FANG (pronounced *Chee Shoo Fong*) saunters into her dressing room in the Kaye Playhouse in midtown Manhattan with an unhurried grace. Dressed casually in a black and gold sweater and warm-up pants, she cradles a huge electric teapot under one arm and carries a tin of jasmine tea in her other hand. The younger members of her Peking Opera Company greet her shyly as her husband, Ding Mei-Kui, directs the stage crew to carry in props and hardshell suitcases of different sizes, containing makeup kits, costume jewelry, and wigs.

The dressing room is crowded, about eight by twelve feet inside, but the door is left wide open. The troupe comes in one or two at a time and shares the tea, which by now steams on the counter off to the side.

"I have no children," she says quietly, and spreads her arms to show her affection for her troupe. She is at once lead

actress, singer, dancer, and consummate *wu-dan*, a Chinese opera singer who plays the roles of women warriors. Often engaging in martial arts, she is elegant but strong, persevering but compassionate, a diligent leader and surrogate mother to all who work alongside her day after day, night after night.

Qi stretches a hairnet over the top of her head and then gently cleanses her face. She powders her skin white with a round pad and, with her fingertips, applies layers of rose-petal makeup to her cheeks and around her eyes. Each step proceeds with a sure hand and an almost whimsical gaze.

In her dressing room, Qi Shu Fang applies the foundation for her stage makeup.

Selecting the right makeup for the role of wu-dan.

"Each night," she explains, "it is different. Both the familiar and the unexpected." While the essential elements of makeup and costume for each role are clearly defined by tradition, the specifics take shape as she transforms her innermost being. With a thin brush, she paints her lips deep red. She carefully inspects the subtle shading and deftly exaggerates the outline of her eyes in black to accentuate the emotion they evoke in the drama of performance. She lifts a yellow flower to the side of her face but then changes her mind, preferring a pale turquoise instead. Then she waits patiently for her dresser to arrive.

Cosmetics, costume jewelry, hairpieces, flowers, and other accessories provide the finishing touches to a performer's transformation into character.

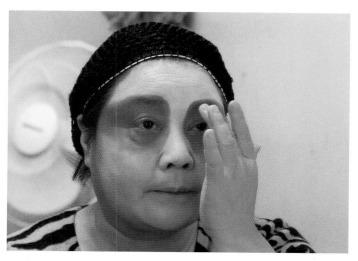

Makeup can change the color, shape, and focus of a face. A performer chooses what to hide, what to alter, what to enhance, what to invent.

After painting her lips a deep red, Qi Shu Fang works on accentuating her eyes.

Black eyeliner on brows and around the eyes helps the audience read a character's expressions and emotions.

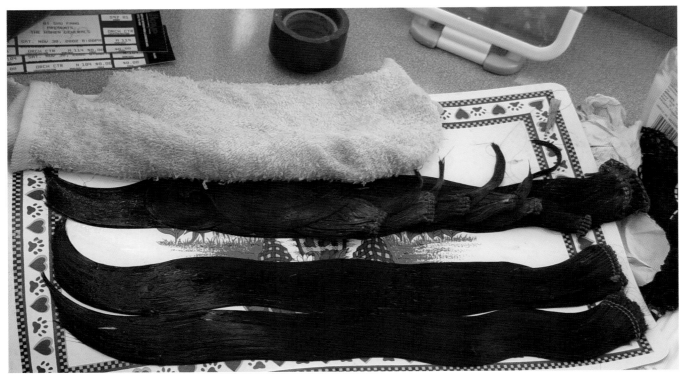

The dresser lays out plaits of black hair soaked in yew sap on Qi Shu Fang's dressing table. Yew sap makes the hair extension sticky enough to hold its shape on her face. It is also gentle on the skin.

A hair bonnet serves to tie back and protect the performer's natural hair.

The bonnet and headscarves are the base to which hair extensions can be attached.

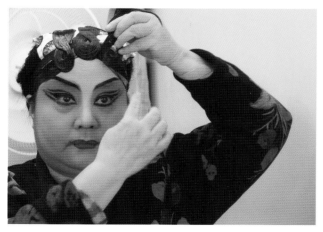

The hair extensions are twisted into shape and attached to the bonnet.

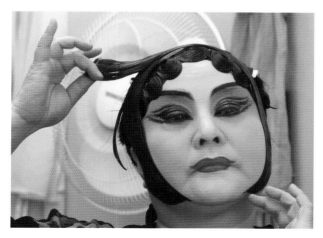

Following the contours of the face, long strands of hair are placed down past the ears and along the jawline.

Another headscarf provides a platform for beads, flowers, and jewels.

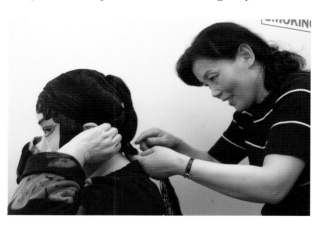

The dresser makes adjustments to the performer's hair.

Baubles and shiny accents are pinned into place.

Qi Shu Fang surveys her completed face and hair.

Qi Shu Fang finishes dressing.

Wang Zhiqiang prepares to play a Song dynasty soldier.

Ge Chen fits the helmet for the character of Wang Wen, the jing *role.*

"All the actors have to study the basic training. But I was very fortunate because Zhang Mei-juan, who was to become my sister-in-law, was a very famous *wu-dan*, and because of her, my exposure and my training were more intense. And because I was born with this voice, I was able to do both the singing and the martial arts. Usually, while still a child, you will be trained to play one particular role. But I went into two types of training at once. I was well rounded.

"I always loved to sing. I started singing when I was very young. I liked all kinds of songs. I sang provincial songs, operatic songs, and was very blessed that I was born with a natural voice. So it was never difficult for me."

The training to become a Beijing Opera performer begins at an early age. Qi Shu Fang, born in 1943, began her studies at age four.

At thirteen, she moved to Shanghai to live with her brother and sister-in-law, who were both active in theater, and enrolled in the Shanghai Theatre Academy.

"I was in the school choir, and I was always like a little tiger, running on a track team—I was very athletic. My brother was already a performer, so even when I was a child, I wanted to go to the theater every night. I had a hard time getting in because I didn't have tickets. But finally, they'd say, 'Okay, your brother's here. Okay, just go upstairs.'

"I came from a family of performers, and I just followed them. The first song I learned was opera. Many of the songs are about the suffering of women, young women, and how they get blamed, and how the virtuous overcome the suffering. The songs come from a wild history, the personal history of the Chinese.

"Ah! Beijing operatic songs are very different from folk songs. Anybody can sing traditional folk songs. They have a low key and a common tune, while operatic songs are highly evolved and highly developed, and written for specific types, like sopranos, tenors, all different kinds of characters."

In Beijing Opera, there are four principal character roles: *dan* (female), *sheng* (male), *chou* (clown), and *jing* (painted face). Usually, actors dedicate themselves to a single type of role and, over the course of their training, become further specialized. In the *dan* role, an actor may become

The finale of Women Generals of the Yang Family. *Left to right: Ren Yucheng as Jia Tinggui, Ma Lianzhi as Seven Wido, Yu Cun as Princess Cai, Zhang Qiuwei as She Taijun, Qi Shu Fang as Mu Gui Ying, and Yuan Xinling as Yang Wen Guang.*

Qi Shu Fang. Publicity photo, Shanghai, 1983.

From left to right: Premier Zhou Enlai, Chairman Mao Zedong, and Qi Shu Fang after her performance as Chang Bao, the hunter's daughter, in Taking Tiger Mountain. *Beijing, China, 1959.*

hua-dan (vivacious young woman), *wu-dan* (martial arts woman), *quing-yi* (refined woman), or *dao-ma-dan* (blade and horse woman). It was only because of Qi's exceptional voice and exemplary skill in martial arts that she was able to master both the *hua-dan* and *wu-dan* roles.

Originating during the Tang Dynasty (618–907), Chinese opera flourished under the Yuan Dynasty (1271–1368) and the Ming Dynasty (1368–1644). It is an ancient art in which singing is supplemented by spoken dialogue, mime, acrobatics, and martial arts.

Until 1949, when the Communists came to power, Beijing Opera was considered a masculine art form, developed by and for male performers. All female roles were played by men imitating women, and thus, when Qi first began to learn opera, she was taught to perform as a woman imitating a man imitating a woman.

"When I was going to school, I was a very recognizable student. I was considered of high caliber, to such an extent that the principal wrote an opera for me that's called *The Three Battles Against Zhang Yue-e.*"

In 1959, Qi was invited to participate in China's largest festival of theatrical performances, organized to celebrate the tenth anniversary of the founding of the People's Republic.

"My performance won first prize and was seen by Chairman Mao Zedong and Premier Zhou Enlai. Chairman Mao even gave me some advice on how to change the script. So when I went back to school, I told the principal, and we adopted the changes that Chairman Mao gave us. This was a traditional Beijing Opera. That was before the Cultural Revolution. I was only sixteen."

Qi Shu Fang as Chang Bao in Taking Tiger Mountain, *1972.*

During the Cultural Revolution, Beijing Opera underwent numerous changes. The traditional repertory was narrowed to eight "model" or "revolutionary" operas that were sanctioned and presented for productions on stage and in film across China.

"I was chosen by Madame Jiang Qing, the wife of Chairman Mao, to play the lead in *Taking Tiger Mountain by Strategy (Zhiqu weihushan)*. She liked that I was rather chubby, with a chubby face, and I was like a little tiger, and after searching throughout the whole nation, she picked me to play this young star. She liked my voice, and she also thought I was very athletic."

Qi Shu Fang (center) as Chang Bao in the movie version of Taking Tiger Mountain, *circa late 1960s.*

Qi's performance in *Taking Tiger Mountain* made her famous, and she was granted membership in the prestigious Shanghai Beijing Opera Theater *(Shanghai jingju yuan)*.

Today, she recalls, "I began touring around the world when I was twenty. I'd been to Luxembourg, Germany, France, Japan, and many other places. When I came to America in 1988, I felt that I had traveled to so many countries and the only place I hadn't been was America. And I wanted to bring my art to America. A lot of people ask me, why did I come to the United States, especially considering that I had achieved such a high level of recognition already. I just felt that I wanted to spread my wings and bring my art to America, a place I had never been.

"At the time, China was opening up communications with the United States, and I applied for a visa. I got here, and I never went back."

Qi Shu Fang as the Egret Queen, the wu-dan *role, in a touring production of* The Flaming Phoenix, *1986.*

Qi settled in New York City, but found her life in America much more challenging than she had expected. Like most Beijing Opera performers trained after 1949, she was considered by some as "uncultured" or "uneducated," having earned only the equivalent of a junior high school diploma.

"I was very fortunate in China because I was first and foremost an artist. Artists were given privileges and opportunities other people did not have. I was actually appreciated by the government for my work. We were like ambassadors

Above: Cast members from The Monkey and the Iron Fan Princess. *Left to right: Li Jinhong as the Ox King; Qi Shu Fang as the Iron Fan Princess; Zhang Dejun as the Wolf Spirit; and Ding Mei-Kui, Qi's husband, as the Monkey King. Toronto, Canada, 2004.*

Right: Qi Shu Fang playing the hua-dan *role of Chen Miaochang, alongside the boatman from a touring production of* Autumn River, *1987.*

of the culture, sending a good message about the country. I wasn't much affected by politics. I was a very naive artist with one single goal: to contribute my art to the people."

Over the last two decades, Qi has struggled to fulfill her dream of performing and advancing Beijing Opera in America. She and her husband founded the Qi Shu Fang Beijing Opera Company in 1988 in New York City. Through the years, she has managed to attract some of the most talented actors and musicians coming from China. Most of these, like her, live in New York City, though some travel from surrounding states to perform with her. Qi is now able to earn a livelihood teaching and performing Beijing Opera. She and her husband manage all operations of their company. Their home in Queens doubles as a rehearsal space, and Qi often provides meals for her actors during performances. Ding, in addition to all his other tasks in rehearsal and performance, also arranges for theater rentals, designs posters, and sells tickets.

About her life in America, Qi remains determined. "I like it here very much. Beijing Opera can have a strong base in New York. I help a lot of the young performers come here. It's very difficult for Chinese immigrants. And we wanted to try to maintain the same kind of artistic integrity and the same kinds of professional standards in America that we did in China."

When asked how she feels, she pauses and says with distinct self-assurance, "Like Mu Gui Ying . . . a heroine," the role she is to play in this evening's performance of the *Women Generals of the Yang Family*.

"I hope that, having been given this recognition in America, I'm able to go back to China and show them how much I have achieved here. I maintain close connection with my friends and the artistic community in China, and they are waiting for me to go home and to put on a big show."

Qi Shu Fang as Mu Gui Ying after the victory over the invaders in Women Generals of the Yang Family. *Kaye Playhouse, New York, 2002.*

Ralph W. Stanley

Boat Builder

Overleaf: Ralph W. Stanley in his boat-building shop, Southwest Harbor, Maine.

Above: A view of Southwest Harbor, Mount Desert Island, Maine, 2004. Ralph W. Stanley's boat-building shop is located in the twin yellow buildings on the left side of the photo.

BY THE END OF MARCH, when the warm air settles on the still-frigid Atlantic Ocean, "the fog comes to Bar Harbor," Ralph W. Stanley says as he leans back in his kitchen chair. "And it dissipates the snow faster than the rain. It stays foggy most of the day, but not enough to keep the lobster boats and the fishermen off the water."

Stanley grew up in Southwest Harbor, on the island of Mount Desert, Maine, and has lived his whole life on the state's rocky coast, surrounded on three sides by the mountains of Acadia National Park. "In the 1940s," he says, "the harbor was ringed with boat builders—big shops, medium-size shops, one-man shops, one-man-and-his-son shops—all churning out boats for fishermen and yachtsmen."

In the past, the coastal towns of Maine were home to large numbers of inshore commercial fishermen and "rusticators," well-to-do people from other parts of the country who vacationed there during the summer months. Boat shops, serving both of these groups, were common. Generally, the boat builders used woods native to the state, principally cedar and oak, but for luxury yachts, they often imported tropical hardwoods such as mahogany and teak.

"As a boy, I used to go around the boat yards. I didn't say anything or ask anything. I just took it all in. Stand back and watch and you find out more. That's how I learned to build wooden boats. I was fascinated by boats, how they ride on the water, sit on the water, the motion, everything. I was

Top: Ralph W. Stanley on his lobster boat. Southwest Harbor, Maine, 1998.

Bottom: Two boats crafted by Ralph, the Acadia *and the* Endeavor, *under sail.*

Above left: Ralph W. Stanley works on the Endeavor, *a Friendship sloop. Beside him is the hull of the* Poor Richard, *a recreational motorboat. Southwest Harbor, Maine, 1979.*

Above right: Ralph works on the Poor Richard. *Beside him is the* Endeavor, *showing the ribbands, which hold the shape of the hull in place until the ribs are attached. Southwest Harbor, Maine, 1979.*

probably five or six when I started making little boats from the scraps of wood I found lying around. They were pretty crude. Anything that would float made me happy. I'd nail together and shape out a steamboat with a smokestack or something like that. I used to rig them up with sails. Some had a single mast, some two."

Although the work of builders who lived near each other was often similar, individuals had their own distinctive styles that had to do with hull shape and the way they finished out their boats. "The old-time builders I knew as a boy," Ralph says, "they built on their own model and wouldn't build on anyone else's. They made a half model—one side of a boat— so that they could see the shape of it. They would put the model together with wooden pegs and take it apart. Then they'd measure the dimensions so that they could get the right scale and proportion to build the boat. Each man took great pride in his own model, and they were always experimenting, playing, trying to improve their design."

When Stanley was about nine years old, he started help-

ing his father, who was a lobsterman and skipper of a yacht for summer residents in and around Southwest Harbor. "He handed me a broom and a brush, and I worked with him to paint the hull."

During his high school years, World War II was raging abroad, and Stanley's enthusiasm for boat building grew as the number of builders helping with the war effort increased in Southwest Harbor. "Many of the builders," Stanley recalls, "worked in the construction of large fishing boats, called draggers, and after the war, the boat builders shifted their attention to smaller lobster and pleasure boats."

Stanley wanted a boat for himself, but couldn't afford to buy one. "About the only way I could get one was to build it. So I gathered up some materials and got it started. I worked a little bit that summer and got enough money to buy the materials. And I got it planked up that winter, so the frame was covered, and the next summer I worked again, got money enough to finish it and make a down payment on an engine.

Above left: Ralph's assistant works on rebuilding the Pegasus *for the Corinthian Yacht Club of Marblehead, Massachusetts, circa 1980s.*

Above right: Ralph sands a model of the Endeavor, *2004.*

Top left: It took Ralph two winters to complete this lobster boat, the first boat he built for a paying customer, 1952.

Top right: The second boat Ralph built was also a lobster boat, 1953.

Bottom: Ralph W. Stanley, age twenty, rowing a dinghy, a small boat used to get from dock or shore to boats moored out in the harbor.

"I built that first boat from a half model. The scale was three-quarters of an inch to one foot. Normally, it'd be one inch to one foot [meaning that if the half model was 28 inches, the boat would be 28 feet long], but my drawing board was too small for that. So I had to improvise. It was a typical lobster boat. I worked two winters to make that first one, from about the first of November until the last of March, something like that. The boat was planked with cedar on an oak frame and keel [the main structural element of a boat stretching along the center line of its bottom from the bow to the stern].

"After I got the first boat done, I thought, 'I'll never have the courage to start another one.' I was so glad to get it done. And then two months later, a fellow came along and wanted me to build him a boat, and I couldn't wait to get started again. And I've been doing it ever since."

Building a boat can take six to nine months or longer. The work is slow, sometimes tedious, and physically demanding. When he wasn't working, Stanley says, he "took up the fiddle" around the age of twenty, and as a pastime, began playing traditional tunes he remembered from his

Ralph W. Stanley at work on a set of line plans in his kitchen, 2004.

childhood, such as "A Bicycle Built for Two" and "She'll Be Coming Round the Mountain." While he enjoyed the quiet time practicing by himself and honing his skills, he also liked playing for his family and jamming with friends.

In designing his boats, Stanley starts by drawing scaled-down "line plans" on paper or by carving scaled-down half-hull models. Then he draws out, or "lofts," the boat's full-scale lines on the floor of his shop. This drawing provides a full-size pattern for the boat to be built. Half models and

Planing a piece of wood.

The Dorothy Elizabeth, *a twenty-eight-foot schooner, under construction, 1997.*

The ribs of a twenty-eight-foot lobster boat in progress.

At work on the Acadia *in Ralph's shop, 1998.*

The Ralph W. Stanley, *a boat built for a customer by Ralph W. Stanley, and now moored off the island of Sardinia, Italy.*

Friendship sloop races. Rockland, Maine, 1998.

drawings are tools to guide the boat builder in the creation of patterns for sections of the boat. In Maine, large boats are normally built in an upright position.

"Building a boat's a challenge, and I like the challenge," says Ralph, "and I like the feeling of accomplishing something. I used to build a lot of lobster boats, and it was a good feeling to build a lobster boat because a man was using that boat and making a living with it, and it would benefit the whole economy. And it was real, you know; the boat was out there working in all kinds of weather, and it had to be built good, and you put a lot of effort into making it solid and seaworthy."

Over the years, Stanley has built approximately seventy traditional boats, from small sailboats to large offshore lobster boats, most of which are still in use. In addition to fishing boats, he has also made a number of pleasure craft. These include engine-powered pleasure boats derived from the lobster boat hull form and single-masted sailing vessels called

Friendship sloops. Stanley liked to build Friendship sloops. "These sloops were originally built in the coastal town of Friendship, Maine, and in later years, they took the name Friendship sloop. But they were built all along the Maine coast, with little variation between different localities. Back in the 1880s, they were used by commercial fishermen, but as time went on, they were called sloop boats or yacht boats because the summer rusticators would come and hire a fisherman to sail them in his sloop." By the 1960s and 1970s, recreational sailors had revived interest in the Friendship sloop, and Stanley became well known for his work restoring old sloops and building new ones in the old style.

"Building wooden boats is like climbing a still-growing tree where you never get to the top. I wouldn't want to be stuck at any point in the process. I keep finding new ways of doing things and new things to do. You can always improve—you're always looking to improve."

Above left: The Summer Joy, *a nineteen-foot sloop built by Ralph W. Stanley, with auxiliary power from an electric motor. The mast is not yet stepped. Southwest Harbor, Maine, 1998.*

Above right: The Annie T, *a twenty-six-foot pleasure lobster boat, built in 1963 by Ralph W. Stanley, owned by Peter Forbes. Southwest Harbor, Maine, 1998.*

Above left: Ralph with his fiddle, 1998.

Above right: Ralph W. Stanley prepares a sail of the Endeavor, *readying the boat for the Friendship sloop races in Rockland, Maine, 1998.*

In recent years, Stanley has continued to design boats but has slowed down considerably. "My oldest son, Richard, runs the shop now. I have four children, two boys and two girls, and my oldest daughter, Nadine, keeps the books for the company. My youngest son, Edward, went to MIT and studied naval architecture. Now he puts my designs in the computer, and that saves us a lot of time and effort. My oldest son is also doing most of the physical work in the boat yard. I'm semi-retired now."

While Stanley seldom works in his boat shop anymore, he still loves the open sea. When the weather breaks around the end of June, Stanley takes his lobster boat, the *Seven Girls*, out and putters around in the harbor. "I go in my lobster boat to see the Friendship sloop races, but back when I had my own Friendship sloop that I built myself, I used to sail out and see how far I could go and not be able to hear the sounds of humanity. But I never could quite get away from it. There was always an airplane going over, a truck in the distance, or a motor or something that I could hear. I couldn't get away from civilization. I'd go out five or six miles maybe. And even if I couldn't hear anything, I'd still see a vapor trail from an airplane or something. Oh, gosh, I don't know. I just like being out on the water. You're by yourself, and there's a certain amount of solitude to it."

Ralph W. Stanley pulls away from his own lobster boat, the Seven Girls, *in a dinghy. The* Seven Girls *serves as the committee boat for the Friendship sloop races in Southwest Harbor and Rockland, Maine.*

Eva Castellanoz

CORONA MAKER

Overleaf: Eva Castellanoz with some of her handmade flowers.

Above: Eva Castellanoz's house and garden. Nyssa, Oregon.

AT SUNRISE, EVA CASTELLANOZ sits at her kitchen table and looks out the window in front of her. Facing east, she watches the sun break above the horizon and sips the violet tea she grows in her garden. As the light brightens, the landscape fills with locust and oak trees. In the distance are orchards heavy with peaches and plums in the summer, apples in the fall. As a child, Eva was taught that "the aurora borealis just before sunrise clears your mind, gets you ready for learning through the day. The sunrise is healing. The sunrise brings the promise of a present each day. The sunrise opens the present of your life, whatever is going to happen, good or bad. It is your present."

She stands and heads out to see her birds in the aviary adjacent to her house. The parakeets, doves, finches, and button-quail call out to her for food. After feeding the birds, she ambles into her garden and speaks softly about her life.

"I was born in Mexico in 1932 in the state of Guanajuato. My daddy's name was Fidel Silva, and my

Eva in her aviary.

mama was Conchita. They're both departed from this world. My daddy was Azteca, and my mama was Otomi. They were both of Indian descent. I was brought by my parents to the United States at the age of three and raised in Pharr, Texas.

"We stayed on the farm in Pharr until I was about fifteen years old, and then we traveled to Clarendon, to Amarillo, and to other places. I can't remember all the names. We would follow the cotton and the watermelon and cantaloupe harvests and then go back to the farm in Texas.

"Then we started coming to Nyssa, Oregon. When we settled in Oregon, it must have been 1959. I was already married. I had gotten married when I was seventeen.

Eva dips a tissue-paper flower into a small pan of melted wax.

"My husband's name is Teodoro Castellanoz. He is a very beautiful, intelligent, hard-working man. I was probably twenty-five years old when he took me to Mexico. That was my first time ever going back there. And out on the street, there was a vendor who had three stones, and in the middle was this *aparato* [apparatus]. It was just a can of oil with a wick, and he had a pot of wax on top of it, and he was making *azahares*. I begged my husband to stop right there because I wanted to see how they were being made. My parents had always talked to me about the *azahar*, but I had never seen one made out of wax. The *azahar* is the bud of the orange blossom. It is not open. It is pure, closed, untouched. That's the Mexicano symbol of purity—of virginity. And from then on, I kept the symbolism of the *azahar* in my heart. I came back and did it my way. I taught myself to make the *azahar* like I saw it made.

"You take little tiny pieces of paper and twist them until they're hard. Then you dip them in wax. You dip each little piece, and dip it and dip it until it forms a little bud on the tip of the twisted paper. Then you fashion it into a *corona*—a crown. The *coronas* are circular—a symbol of the cycle of life—around and around and around."

In Mexico, the *coronas* are used at baptisms, Holy Communions, weddings, and *quinceañeras*, girls' fifteenth-birthday celebrations. They are often placed on the tombs of the dead, after someone is buried, and on November 2, when the Day of the Dead is celebrated.

"For the cemetery, I make just flowers. Just big flowers. Any kind of flower that the person wants.

"For the baptism, I put a little bunch of *azahares* as the

symbol on the side of the little cap. For the first Holy Communion, I make the *corona*, and it's either a little round circle or just a half circle for the top of a girl's head. Those are made out of the little orange buds, pure orange buds—no flowers.

"For weddings, I make all kinds of flowers. I can make roses, carnations, orchids, any kind of flower—lilies, pansies, any kind of flower.

"Now, for the *quinceañera*, I can make any kind of flower that the girl wants. It used to be that it was mostly *azahares* for the wedding and *quinceañera* and first Holy Communion. But we evolve with the times. Now people ask me to put in flowers, so I put in flowers."

The *quinceañera* is a rite of passage that introduces a young woman to the community of adults. The *corona* is central to the aesthetics of the *quinceañera* event, as necessary as the ring to a wedding.

Above left: Eva's showcase of bouquets for all occasions.

Above right: Young bride Patricia Fraga holds one of Eva Castellanoz's creations. The groom is Eva's son, Martin Castellanoz.

Above left: Elsa Lazo checks her daughter's makeup while madrina *Ofelia Franco fixes Elnoris Lazo's hair in preparation for the young woman's* quinceañera.

Above right: A quinceañera corona *handcrafted by Eva Castellanoz.*

"I didn't have a *quinceañera* in church because we couldn't get to town. I had it at my home in the evening.

"On the day of my *quinceañera*, I got up at about five or five-thirty in the morning. My mother helped me bathe in one of those long, old tubs with all this beautiful herbal water. Then she put my hair up. Now I laugh because I see how the girls make their curls with a curling iron. But what my mother used were these old coffee bags that had wire enclosures. She rolled my hair onto these wires and then folded them over on each other to make my hair curl. She just left my hair that way until it dried.

"My mother made me a dress out of bleached flour sacks. It was just a plain dress. And I wore my old little sandals.

"I didn't have any *madrinas* or *quinceañera* maids or

what they call *damas*. A *madrina* is a sponsor, somebody who comes and helps you with your hair or buys you a dress or shoes. Everything is supposed to be new. You are to start wearing things that you have never worn—like earrings, your first bracelet, your first pendant. I didn't have all of that when I was young because we were illegal immigrants. We didn't get to meet many people. We were all poor on the farm.

"The *dama* is just a young girl like you who stands by you in the hope and in the promise that she'll be with you for your whole life. The *damas* are supposed to be your best friends, but I didn't have any.

"My ceremony began with a prayer at about seven in the evening. And my mama and daddy said, 'Now you're becoming a woman. These are the things a woman must do.' Then my daddy placed the *corona* on me. Some of the guests cried.

"After Daddy presented me with the *corona*, I sat down and we ate *mole*. My mother made the *mole*. We gave thanks, and that was it. There was no dance. It was very simple but very, very beautiful and touching. We were taught by deeds, not by words, to appreciate whatever smallest thing we had. I was so proud. I had the most special feeling."

The basic materials of Castellanoz's art are simple and inexpensive: typing paper or crepe paper, wax candles, scissors, glue, and wire. She begins by cutting out the petals, forming them into the shape of the desired flower, and binding them with wire or glue. Then she melts candles and dips the paper in the wax. Several applications and lots of time might be required for the proper effect. When the flower has taken shape, she dips her finger, a piece of cotton, a tissue, or

Top: Elnoris Lazo wearing her quinceañera corona, *made by Eva Castellanoz.*

Bottom: Three quinceañera damas.

Top: *Eva Castellanoz at work at the local community center, Nyssa, Oregon.*

Center: *The tools of Eva's trade: tissue-paper petals and hot wax kept at just the right temperature and consistency.*

Bottom: *Eva uses a scissors blade to give body to a single disk of cut paper.*

brush into the melted colored wax and applies a touch of pink or blue to the edges of a petal to make them look like real flowers. Finally, she arranges the flowers for the *corona* or bouquet into the desired arrangement.

"Now I use wires. Before, I made little papers that I rolled in my fingers—just roll and roll them till they're really tight, then keep dipping the little end into the wax until it's like a little teardrop. That's the bud.

"I connect them together with tape. It takes a while, but they are so beautiful. I have had to make long *coronas*, for a bride or for a *quinceañera*. It may contain five hundred *azahares*. And I have made a *corona* with as many as a thousand *azahares*. I love them. When they are that long, they drape down. They go from shorter to longer, up to halfway down the chest. They drape around the contours of your face, like a frame. It's just indescribable. They're beautiful.

"Sometimes, to add color, I can bleed the paper, especially Mexican paper, because paper from here doesn't do that. But when I am able to get my hands on Mexican paper, what I do is get alcohol, cut my petals and put them on a plate and let them take a little drink of the alcohol, and that bleeds the color out so that I will have a dark center and a light outer part to the flower. It can be red; it can be blue, whatever. Then I put my flower together and dip it into the wax. I just use the wax from candles that I buy. I melt them, and now I have an electric pot. Years ago, I melted them on the *comal* [stove]. You heat the wax to 120 or 125 degrees, and then you just dip your flower, shake most of the wax off, let it dry for a few seconds, and dip it again. I do it three times, and it forms the most beautiful flowers."

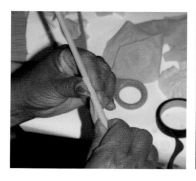

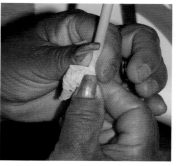

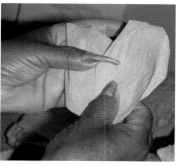

Eva wraps a paper disk around a knitting needle to give it shape.

By sliding and scrunching the two ends of the paper together along the needle, Eva gives a paper disk texture.

Two prepared paper disks.

Folded together and pinched at one end, a pair of paper petals forms the heart of a flower.

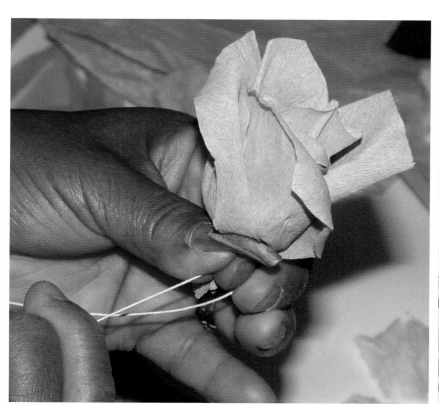

String holds the arranged petals in place.

A paper flower gets a coat of melted wax.

The sign outside Eva's home: Flowers by Eva: Corsages, Bouquets, Centerpieces, and Flower Arrangements.

As the only *corona* maker in the region, Eva was sought out by parents and families who journeyed hundreds of miles to consult her. She has since demonstrated the making of the *corona* in festivals and school programs, and has participated in workshops and other educational efforts, both within her Mexican American community and for the general public.

"When I started making the *corona*, I changed. I had been a young woman who hardly ever talked. Now I even talk to my hair. But before, I was just like a little shadow. I guess I communicated with the world through all the beautiful things that I had, that I used to see my parents do.

"Every morning, we went to work very early with our parents. Then we'd run home, wash up, go to school, and come back and go to work some more. We'd make bundles of radishes or baby onions, or we'd pick fruit or vegetables for the stores. We were always involved in what our parents were doing. The only time we were away from them was to go to school. My parents were so, so fabulous. Even though

we were very, very poor, my parents took time with us. They wanted us with them.

"I was constantly awed by my daddy. I always saw lots of love in his face when he woke up in the morning and got ready to go to work.

"When Mama wasn't working on the farm, she had to work in a restaurant, making tortillas, but she wouldn't go unless her two little girls went with her. My mama was very famous around the Valley for making beautiful tortillas. Everybody wanted her to make tortillas. She made them fast, and if you wanted them really small, she would make them really small. If you wanted them huge, she would make them huge. She could make a tortilla so that when she put it on the *comal*, it was like blowing up a balloon. It would puff up, and when you got it off of the *comal*, you could pry it apart and have two very thin tortillas.

Above left: A colorful assortment of tissue-paper flowers made by Eva Castellanoz.

Above right: Finishing off the stem of a wax flower.

A wedding bouquet featuring white roses and azahares.

"I loved to play around my mom while she worked. She would give me little pieces of dough so that I could try to make tortillas.

"Oh, my parents would make us toys and just about everything we had out of whatever they could. We would always see them doing things, and we would just ask, 'What are you doing?' They'd say, 'Oh, we're doing this. Would you like to try? Would you like to watch?' My childhood was magical to me.

Eva watches a young girl try her hand at forming a paper flower at the Nyssa Learning Center, Nyssa, Oregon.

"I remember seeing my daddy go to the pumpkin patch and get the big leaves to make us little flutes. He would make us toys from things he took off the trees or off the plants and rocks. He would take us to the river and say, 'What is the rock? Do you think it's a boy, or do you think it's a girl? Hold it. Touch it. What is it?' We would go out to gather wood for the week, and he would find things to feed us out in the woods. And I thought, 'Wow, how wonderful. We don't bring anything, yet we're eating.' My daddy knew plants and roots. He could start a fire with no matches. He was just great and could do so many things not many people knew.

"Mama would sew our clothes. She would quilt for the lady of the farm. And she would make little chickens for us with cotton and little pieces of wood. She'd paint the fleece of the cotton with yolk to make them look like little chickens.

"When we were sick, Mama would go out to the woods to find all these plants and herbs. She did a lot of healing.

Above: Eva demonstrates one step in the flower-making process to a curious observer. Nyssa Learning Center, Nyssa, Oregon.

Right: Eva Castellanoz is invited into schools to speak about her traditional art. Here, a volunteer models one of Eva's coronas while Eva listens to what the children have to say.

She was a *curandera*, and my daddy was a *curandero*. They both knew a lot about herbs. They both came from people who were healers. To me, it was just like magic.

"My parents would gather us and make these little bonfires and get these seeds off some trees that grow wild in Texas—or garbanzos or pumpkin seeds—and roast them. We would sit around our little fire and they would explain to us a lot of our traditions. I chose not to forget them, and I still keep them in my heart. I think they're good. They're remedies that heal a lot of hurt and a lot of things that happen in our life.

"My parents would talk to us about how they used to live in Mexico and how they wanted us not to live that way. They just encouraged us always to do better. Always do better.

"I love to be busy. I love what I do. My own family, and many other children have learned to make the *corona* from me. They call me a folk artist. Everybody likes my paper and wax flowers and my *azahares*, so that's what I do. This is the way I lived around my root family, my parents. I just love being creative, and so I share all I know with the children.

"Children. They are the most wonderful treasures that we have."

Eva Castellanoz stands beside a spectacular display of her handmade blooms.

DOROTHY TRUMPOLD

WEAVER

Overleaf: Dorothy Trumpold at her loom.

Right: East Amana, 2002.

DRIVING SOUTH from Cedar Rapids, Iowa, to Amana, the flat prairie lands give way to rolling hills that slope through the late autumn haze and fall away into the soft curves of the sprawling Iowa River. The seven Amana Colonies have a deep history that spans more than a century and still emanates from the land, the weathered barns, and Civil War–era homes. The name *Amana*, Dorothy Trumpold says, means "to remain true" and comes from the Song of Solomon in the Old Testament of the Bible.

Dorothy Schuerer Trumpold was born on September 22, 1912, in her family home in East Amana, Iowa. She has lived her entire life in the Amana Colonies, which have a unique social and religious history. Settlers of these communities, often confused with the Amish, came from Germany and

were members of the Community of True Inspiration, a Lutheran sect founded in 1714 and based on the belief that God can communicate through an inspired individual. The group first moved to Ebenezer, New York, and then to Iowa in 1855.

"When I was born, East Amana still had a communal way of life. I grew up in a house shared by my immediate family, as well as my grandparents and other relatives. All property belonged to a common fund, and everyone worked for the common good and, in turn, received food, clothing, and lodging. The Community of True Inspiration instilled me with the values and resolve that have guided my life and work.

Above left: Wedding procession at the Amana Colonies. High Amana, Iowa, August 22, 1907.

Above right: Dorothy Schuerer (right) and her sister, Louise. Marengo, Iowa, circa 1919.

Interior of the Amana cooper shop, circa 1940s.

My father, Benjamin Schuerer, was a cooper. He made barrels, buckets, wooden sinks, bathtubs. We had real long, big bathtubs. They were used in the wash houses. Every home had a wash house where there was a big kettle with a fire underneath to heat the water. There was no electricity, no water heaters, or anything like that. In the summer, we could take a bath outside. But in the winter, we'd heat the water on the stove. Everybody had a wood stove. And every family got so many loads of wood for free each winter.

"My mother, Catherine, was a seamstress and a kitchen worker. She got up every morning before six and helped the other ladies peel potatoes in the community kitchen. By six o'clock in the morning, the cooks had to have two big pans of

Interior of a communal kitchen house. East Amana, circa 1910. The woman in the foreground is Dorothy's aunt, Helen Schuerer. Seated in the background are Dorothy's grandmother, Dorothea Foerstner Hess, and her grandmother's sister, Carolina Pfeffer.

fried potatoes ready when everyone came in to eat. For breakfast, they usually had bread and butter, fried potatoes, coffee, and milk. For lunch, at noon, they always had some kind of soup—barley, rice, tomato, pea, or dumpling. It was different every day. And they might have cheese, maybe a hard-boiled egg, bread and butter, and coffee. Then she'd get the vegetables ready. She'd do whatever had to be done. There were four kitchen houses in East Amana, one on each corner. It was just a little square town. At that time, there were about one hundred people living in East Amana, and about twenty-five or thirty people went to each kitchen house for all their meals.

"As a girl, I learned knitting, crocheting, and embroidery. I spent time with my grandfather, watching him at the loom and helping him prepare shuttles for carpet weaving. I learned to make crocheted, braided, and hooked rugs. By the time I was twelve, I had learned to make my own clothes.

Dorothy Trumpold's maternal grandfather, Louis Hess, circa 1915–1920.

"My grandfather, Louis Hess, was a carpet weaver, and I loved to watch him weave. He used whatever people brought him. People brought him rags and all the old clothes, sheets, and pillowcases they had, mostly white things. And they cut them into strands and took them to the woolen mill. There they would dye them light brown or dark brown. Sometimes they made them black with stripes. And sometimes they got rags from the mill. That was wool. The rest was usually cotton or blue calico. So that's how my grandfather made the carpets for people's homes."

In 1932, members of the Amana Society voted to dissolve the communal way of life through what was simply called "The Great Change." Individuals were given a share of property ownership, proportionate to their age, the size of their family, and the amount of work contributed to the sustenance of the community. "I worked in the kitchen house until the Change. And, after the Change, I worked at the woolen mill, which by then had been rebuilt. We made ten cents an hour for a long time. I worked in the spinning department, but I didn't stay very long. I got married to Carl Trumpold in 1933. And my sister-in-law and I, we were the only married people there at the woolen mill, so we were the first to get laid off when they didn't have enough orders."

In 1940, Dorothy took over carpet weaving from her ailing grandfather. "I taught myself to weave on my grandfather's loom when he got kind of sick. He was the weaver here, but he couldn't weave anymore. He was worried that somebody might not pick it up because he still had some rags that had to be made into rugs. He couldn't walk very well, and to please him, I tried it. And I liked it. I had fun doing it,

Above left: The East Amana Cemetery, where Dorothy's husband and members of her family are buried.

Above right: Dorothy and Carl Trumpold's wedding photograph, 1933.

Left: Dorothy Trumpold at the cast-iron loom that belonged to her grandfather Louis Hess. East Amana, circa 1940s.

Dorothy spinning warp threads to be used on her loom.

and that's when I started. I began making throw rugs and then for years made full-size room carpets, using the cast-iron loom my family brought from Europe in the 1840s.

"Back then, the loom was across the street, in a little building that was once the night watchman's house. It wasn't until after my husband inherited this house that we moved the loom over here. That's when they split the house. My husband got this part, and his brother got the other part, which they moved across the street. It was originally built in 1860 as a kitchen house and had two big sections, big enough to make two homes.

"A lot of people brought me their own rags at first, and I'd make the rugs for them. They'd give me the size for what they needed, how many strips, and the size of the room. The strips were usually a yard wide back then, and I sewed the strips together to make wall-to-wall carpeting. In about two weeks, I could make a carpet that was nine by twelve feet or larger, maybe sixteen yards. Sometimes I'd work eight to ten hours a day. I know in the summer, I'd go there and work after we had dinner.

"In one bedroom, I used the upholstery material from Studebaker cars—a lady from Indiana sent them to me. Somebody in her family was working there, and they had leftovers when they cut out the seats of the cars. The material was made out of wool.

"For the rugs in my living room, we bought a lot of coats and stuff at the Salvation Army, Goodwill, and other thrift stores. I needed a lot of rags. At that time, when I made the living-room rugs, the earth colors were in style. So, we mostly had tans and browns for that room.

"For the other rooms, I used primarily mill-ends from the woolen mill in Amana. They would sell them for fifty cents a pound. I'd cut them up into rags and sew them into long strips. But at the woolen mill, you couldn't pick the colors. You had to buy whatever they had available. They would put the ends in a sack and sell them by the pound. They had a lot of sheep here in East Amana and a lot of wool. But they had to buy more from farmers and from anyone else they could. I have no idea where they got it all or what kind of dyes they used. Probably, some were natural dyes and some were chemical dyes.

Top: At the sewing machine, joining wool and cotton rags end-to-end to form the long strands, or woof, which will be wound around a shuttle.

Bottom: Detail from one of Dorothy Trumpold's woven rugs.

Cutting wool and cotton remnants into strips.

Sewing the strips end to end.

The lengthening strand of cloth is coiled into a ball at Dorothy's elbow.

A view of the warp threads on Dorothy's loom. Running the length of a rug, the warp forms the basic skeleton between which the long strips of cloth, or woof threads, are woven horizontally.

Winding a strip of cloth onto a shuttle. The shuttle carries the woof threads back and forth between the warp threads.

"Well, I use whatever is handed down, anything you can't wear anymore or can't use anymore. That's what I use for rags. They're fine. You can leave out the parts that are worn and just take the good parts. I mix cotton and wool. But you still have to be careful when you wash the rug. If there's wool in there, it should be washed like wool.

"I start with strips of rags, which I make myself. It depends on the material: cotton, I tear; wool, I cut; some polyester, I cut, but I don't like anything that's knitted. It stretches too much. I cut wool flannel three-quarters of an inch wide and cotton one to one-and-a-half inches wide. I have the feel in my hands, and then I cut it accordingly.

"I sew the ends of the strips together. I lay the ends on top of each other so they overlap about a half inch and sew them together with the electric sewing machine I bought in 1940 from Sears, Roebuck and Company. And when I have a long strip pieced together, I start wrapping it around my hand. I hold one end and keep wrapping until it forms into a big ball. Later on, when I go down to the loom, I unwrap this long strip of rags onto the wood shuttle. There's a little slit in the shuttle where I put one end of the strip so it holds.

"Before I start weaving, I always put about a hundred yards of warp onto the loom. There are 230 warp threads to make a rug that's twenty-seven inches wide. I used to make rugs a yard wide, but that required more warp. For every two inches of warp, there are about fifteen threads.

"When I start the rug, I weave about twelve shots of warp to make the heading for the fringe. Each time I throw the shuttle, I call it a shot. I don't know if that's the right word, but that's what I call it when I throw the shuttle.

With her left hand, Dorothy pulls on the handle of the beater. The beater firmly pushes a newly woven row up against the others, ensuring a tight weave.

"The warp thread that I buy comes in spools, but I have a spinning wheel to wind the warp onto my shuttle. It's a different shuttle than I use for the rags. It's smaller and round, and it has a kind of spool for thread. I buy carpet warp thread from the Newport Loom Company in Washington, Kentucky. They never made the warp thread in Amana. I used to order it from Sears, Roebuck in Chicago, but they don't carry it anymore. The warp comes in all colors. I always use the reddish brown because it matches everything, just about.

"When I finish weaving the rug, I do another twelve shots of warp to make the heading for the fringe on the other end of the rug. I always have one rug on the loom that winds around the wooden beam on the bottom. When I finish a rug, I cut the other one off and leave about four inches of warp for the fringe. Then I take the rug off the loom and tie the fringe with knots to keep it from unraveling.

"What always gets me the most praise is the way I mix colors. I try to use the colors that are in most of the material I use for the rug. Whatever colors are there, I try to match with my stripes. Sometimes I use blue with red, if it matches nice. And sometimes blue and green.

"Nobody has enough material to make the full-size carpets anymore, and probably, they don't have the interest. It's a lot of work.

"I've had a few girls come by over the years who wanted to learn to weave. There's a girl from East Amana, and she's in a 4-H Club and she makes a rug each year to take to the

Above left: A close-up view of two shuttles—one loaded with woof threads—sitting atop the warp threads. Also visible are a section of finished rows and the edge of the beater.

Above right: Detail of Dorothy pulling on the beater to tighten the finished weave.

An array of rugs and carpets woven by Dorothy Trumpold showcases her talent for mixing and matching colors and improvising pleasing patterns.

state fair in Des Moines. She's in high school now and she's come for four years. It usually takes one day to weave, but we made the strips of rags at my house. We sewed them on my machine.

"Her mother even brought her younger brother once. Then I had a girl from Ames. She was already married. She has her own loom now, but she tries all kinds of things.

"I've always loved to weave because there was always a lot of stuff that we just had and could cut into rugs, you know, or weave into rugs. I used just about every piece up.

"I've learned how to picture the rug before it's woven, how it will look. I don't exactly dream about them. Well, sometimes when I go to bed, I think about what I have to do tomorrow. I have to do that and do this. And I wake up and know what to do . . . well, kind of, yeah, sure."

Dorothy Trumpold. East Amana, Iowa, 2002.

Allison "tootie" Montana

Mardi Gras Indian

Overleaf: Allison "Tootie" Montana, Big Chief, Yellow Pocahontas.

Above: Tootie Montana stands on the front steps of his house. His wife, Joyce, is seated on the porch. New Orleans, 2004.

ON MARDI GRAS MORNING, Allison "Tootie" Montana is up before daybreak. He watches the shadows of the first sun stretch across the pavement outside. He steps onto the stoop of his wood-frame house in New Orleans's Seventh Ward and hears the first Mardi Gras Indians stir. A Spy Boy calls to his Chief, and fifty-one years of his own "masking" flash before him in a collage of syncopated words and images.

Mardi Gras, or Fat Tuesday, is the last day before the beginning of Lent in the Christian calendar. In New Orleans, Mardi Gras is celebrated with costumes, parades, and elaborate festivities. Much of what is known about the Mardi Gras

Tootie Montana with his mother, Alice Montana. New Orleans, 1922.

Indians has been passed on from one generation to the next. By most accounts, the customs associated with masking and costuming Indian began in the 1880s and have their roots in a mix of American Indian, Caribbean, and African traditions.

While the origins of New Orleans are European, predominantly French and Spanish, the slave trade brought thousands of Africans to the city through the ports of the Caribbean. After the Civil War, New Orleans remained an intensely segregated city but grew rapidly, and in 1884, it hosted the celebration of a world's fair, the Cotton

Tootie Montana's grandfather Big Chief Alfred Montana (second from the left) with the queen of the Yellow Pocahontas, his wife, Elnora Montana (third from left). New Orleans, circa 1930s.

Centennial Exposition. That same year, Buffalo Bill's Wild West Show wintered in New Orleans and performed regularly over a four-month period. Some historians believe this show was the genesis of the Mardi Gras Indians, pointing specifically to the name Creole Wild West as the earliest Indian "tribe," though many today, Tootie Montana included, reject the implication that masking Indian was started by or inspired by Buffalo Bill's show.

Tootie says, "My grandmother told me her brother, Becate Batiste, was with the first Mardi Gras Indian tribe, the Creole Wild West, downtown. They had large tribes, about fifteen, seventeen, eighteen. They'd have Big Chief, Second Chief, Third Chief, Trail Chief, Flag Boys, Spy Boys, and Wildman, or Medicine Man. The ladies were called Queens, and they'd have First Queen, Second Queen. They would have a Spy Girl, who used to run out there with the men.

"The Chief during my daddy's time was Robert Sam Tillman Jr., who was known as Brother Timber, and he had the reputation of being the *baddest* on Carnival day, not the prettiest. In Daddy's time, you got your name not by your costume but by how bad you were, how violent. They used to fight. All of the tribes had their own location in the neighborhood where they practiced, and they would plot and plan against each other. When one tribe meets another and that Big Chief can make me kneel down, then that's a disgrace. He tells me, 'Hum Bah.' That means get on your knees. Now, who's going to get on their knees and bow to another man? And I say, 'No Hum Bah.' And when you didn't do it, that's when the fighting broke out. In those days, they used to mask with beautiful silk capes, and when they'd come up to you on the street, they'd be covered up, and when they'd open that cape, a gun would be in their hands.

"In those days long ago, if you turned your back, you might get your head chopped off or split. A song they used to sing a long time ago during my daddy's time was 'Sore, Sore, Sore.' What it meant was that Carnival was over and they had met some tribe and somebody had got hurt. And if your tribe had put some hurt on another tribe, you came back singing that."

For decades, the Mardi Gras Indians practiced and marched in their parades in secrecy. They kept the times and routes they were going to follow private. If you were to go to New Orleans looking for Mardi Gras Indians, you might never find them.

"After World War II, Carnival changed, and the fighting stopped, but the tension is always there. It's like going to a party where somebody can't handle their drink and they're going to make trouble. It's no different for the Indians on Carnival day, except that it's open to the public.

"When I was a kid, the Carnival parade had a sound to it. It had a feeling. You could hear the horse steps. Today they have big rubber tires. When a parade was five or six blocks away, you had that feeling. Years ago you could hear the Indians. They used spangles on their suits.

"Carnival was one day when nobody had to wake you up. Every child in the house (there were ten children in ours) would get up early. If you didn't hear an Indian hollering out there, the smell of the doughnuts my grandmother was making would wake you up. There was potato salad and ham sandwiches and a big pot of cocoa or coffee. There were

Allison "Tootie" Montana (second row, center) with his brother, sister, and first cousins. New Orleans, circa 1928.

Members of the tribe of Monogram Hunters. Left to right: Harold Federson, Joseph Simon, Anna Bee, and Tootie Montana. New Orleans, 1949.

people coming to the house all day. It was one big hell of a good time. It was a day you hated to see the sun set. It was beautiful."

What started Tootie participating in the tradition was that his father "had helped these boys in the Eighth Ward to form a gang. And I told him I wanted to mask, too. Carnival was three weeks away. He said, 'You want to mask? When? Next year?' I said, 'No, this year.' I didn't know what I was doing, but I made a little suit. That was in 1947.

"When I told my mother I was going to mask Indian, she thought I was crazy. She didn't want me to do it. I have a medal, a scapular, in my wallet that my mother pinned on my Indian suit every Carnival. She was a strict Catholic, and a Carnival didn't pass, when she was still alive, that she didn't call later on that night to see if I was all right. Then she could go to bed. She knew how it used to be.

"The song 'Indian Red' was like a hymn that was sung on Mardi Gras morning. When it's being sung, it's beautiful; the men's and women's voices mix together. Before you sing, you make your introduction:

> *Big Chief Yellow Pocahontas*
> *Don't make no bow 'cause I don't know how*
> *From a dump I bust a rump*
> *From Manila I make a caterpillar climb up a wall*
> *And he get to the top and better not fall.*

"See, you put all kinds of rhyme in it. You hit your drum [tambourine] and sing, 'Mah-day two-de fiyo,' and then the crowd comes in. And when my daddy did it, you had women's voices join in. Man, it put tears in your eyes.

Tootie Montana at Yellow Pocahontas practice.
Pauger and Marais Streets, New Orleans,
circa 1960s.

Il yan day, Il yan day
So we are from the nation
The wild, wild creation
Won't you hear me calling
Softly, softly calling
Oh, my Indian Red, my Indian Red.
"And somebody will be singing:
Oh, we kill them dead
Because I love to hear you call my Indian Red.

Young Men's Olympian Social and Pleasure Club. New Orleans, 1981.

Larry Bannock, Big Chief, Golden Star Hunters. Mardi Gras, New Orleans, 1983.

Tootie Montana, Big Chief, Yellow Pocahontas.
Mardi Gras, New Orleans, 1986.

"Now, 'Indian Red' is a song that I used to introduce all the members of my tribe. I get ready to call my Flag Boy and my Spy Boy. And you point, and it looks like he's coming out of your finger if you're doing it right.

"And the Spy Boy shouts, 'Spy Boy, Yellow Pochahontas!' And he gets out on the floor and does his number, and he ends by singing, 'Because I love to hear you call my Indian Red.'

"Then I call the Flag Boy, and I call out everybody in the tribe one by one. And I call the Second Chief, who is my brother, and I give him the tambourine, and he calls me. And after he calls me, he gives me back the tambourine and I wind the song up. I start humming and beat the tambourine fast, and then the song's over.

"I sing it the way my daddy sang it. There's this one Chief, who said every time he saw me, 'Oh, you got to change it.' How you going to change something they say that they were singing before you were born? So I said, 'If you want me to change something, change the suit you make every year. Make a new suit.'

"I traveled all over the city, go maybe fifteen or twenty miles over the course of one day. I'd usually leave from my house by eight A.M. Sometimes, I left at daybreak, or when it was still dark outside. I'd start at the corner of Marais and Pauger Streets. And the whole block was packed with people, waiting to see me come out. I had a route I followed every year. Different people in the community gave you stops, a place, a house. People give you a drink, red beans and rice, if you want. And at the end of the day, all the Indians would meet at Claiborne and Orleans. And we'd hang there until it got dark. Next day, Ash Wednesday, I'd be the first man on the job. Never drive. Never miss a day of work.

"I've masked and made my own costumes for more than fifty years. When it comes to creating, God—the man up there—gives that to you, and I thank Him every night for giving me the knowledge to understand and do so much. When it comes to Indian suits, I design and create just about anything with my own ideas. I don't want what I've seen anywhere else.

"I see it like a picture, and I draw it, and I better draw it fast. The picture starts coming into my head, and I grab a pencil and sketch it right quick. It comes just like a cloud, floats right through my mind and goes on. If I don't bring it into reality, then it's lost.

"My trade helped me with my Indian costumes, and my costumes helped me with my trade. I worked most of my life as a lather. Back then, the old houses around the city were shaped up with wood laths. The lath is a thin strip used

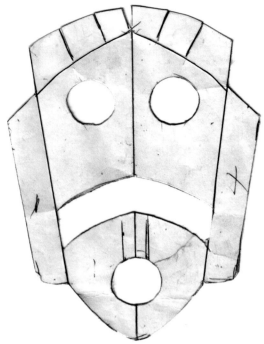

Above left: At home working on design patterns for a Mardi Gras Indian suit, 2004.

Above right: Pattern piece for the suit.

Right: Pattern pieces for the crown.

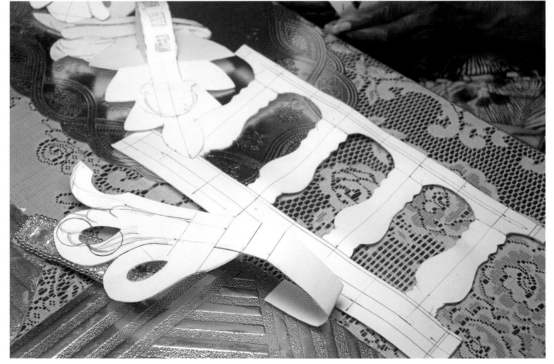

to form a framework for the plaster. The carpenter framed the house, and then I put up the lath on the wall. The lath might be one to two feet, maybe four feet long. I could throw those nails out of my mouth so fast, you couldn't even see them . . . *Tap! Tap! Tap! Tap!* It sounded like I was playing music.

"Later on, they shifted to the metal lath and then to hanging wire. I've always liked building things. I've done a lot of fancy work on buildings—domes, arches, suspended ceilings, stepped-up ceilings, acoustic ceilings. I built the frame and set up the background for the plaster. I did the background for the plaster. I built the frame with metal and wire. I shaped arches and other forms. It's like designing costumes.

"Sometimes it takes weeks, cutting up cardboard, drawing designs. I change my costume every year. If I didn't

Above left: Tootie and his wife, Joyce, piece together the pieces of his Mardi Gras Indian suit, 1996.

Above right: Tootie spreads out a portion of his suit on the kitchen floor to place some decorative detailing, 1991.

Making adjustments and repairs to beadwork on the apron of one of his Mardi Gras Indian suits, 2004.

change my costume, somebody might copy it, and one of these times we'd be out there on the street alike. I throw them off; they never see the same thing twice.

"I couldn't make a suit without Joyce. We've been married since 1958, and for most of those years, I did all the framework, and she did all the fill-in on top of what I designed. I put on the stones, and she sewed every sequin on there with a bead in the middle. I pick the best rhinestones.

"The Uptown Indians use the beaded designs more and the small rhinestones. The Downtown Indians, like myself, stick more to what they now call sequins, but my daddy

Every bead, sequin, or jewel on a suit made by Tootie is sewn into place by hand.

called them fish scales. They were real scales back then; sequins are made out of plastic. The scales had changeable colors when the sun hit them. Today I use some beads, but I prefer the big stones to the small ones.

"Uptown, they use a lot of ribbon. I don't use ribbon. Black Benny from Downtown was the first to use feathers and plumes. Black Benny was Chief of the One Hundred and One Indian tribe. He used to mask with my daddy. He was Second Chief with my daddy when my daddy was Big Chief of the Yellow Pocahontas, which is the tribe I have now. Black Benny came out one year in red, loaded with pins and

Allison "Tootie" Montana. Mardi Gras, New Orleans, 1995.

pompoms. He was pretty in those times. He had short red plumes. And the next year, he came out in an identical suit, but with white plumes.

"The year after that the Chief of the White Eagles, who used to be my competition, had his Uptown Indians come out with blue and white plumes. And everybody Uptown has been using plumes ever since. Plumes are a cover-up. I'd rather use feathers. I used to get turkey feathers. I'd go around to the places that I knew sold chickens and turkeys and I'd talk to the guy and he'd put them up for me.

"When I used the turkey feathers, I'd have to dye them myself. The turkey feathers are gray and have stripes in them. A lot of guys used them natural, just the way they were. But then when the different-colored feathers started coming out, we started buying them. Feathers have always been my thing. Everybody in my tribe wore feathers. We had a different style of sewing. It was a lot of work. When I was stringing my feathers, I had to make a loop on each one. When I pulled my needle through, I pulled it back and looped it, and that locked the feather in. Then I wrapped them so they stayed flexible in the wind, especially on the headpiece, which we called the crown. On the back of the crown, you can make a double row or a triple with different wing feathers. Some years I used plume tips. The feathers come from the wings, and the plumes come from the tail.

"There always has been a conflict between the Uptown Indians and the Downtown Indians. Always been a controversy over that, you see? So here's what you want to do: you know your people in that other chief's territory and make him look bad around his neighborhood where everybody thinks he's so pretty. And here come Tootie Montana. They could say to them, 'Woo, boy, who he is!' Say, 'Man, that's Chief Tootie Montana. That's the chief that's from Downtown.' Oh, man, woo, Lord, it's a thrill when you go Downtown and make all those Uptown chiefs look bad in their territory, where everybody go up there think they're so pretty.

Tootie fits the cuffs of his granddaughter Chelsi's Mardi Gras Indian suit, while Joyce holds Chelsi's crown. New Orleans, 2004.

"The Indian suit I wore was hot and heavy. I had to lower that crown down on my head with a rope. I had about three or four people to help.

"I used to work on my Indian suit every day. I'd go to work and get home that evening. I start sewing. The closer Carnival gets, the more I sew. I might go to bed at 2:00 A.M. and get up at 5:45 A.M. The week of Carnival, I might get two hours' sleep. The weekend before, I didn't go to bed. I work on my suit all night Friday. All day Saturday I buy more material—stones, feathers, whatever I need. I sew all night Saturday. Sunday we have practice. All night, I sew. Go to work on Monday. Get off that streetcar running. Sew all night Monday. Don't stop sewing until I put that suit on. And sometimes they were still sewing after I put that suit on.

"I've decided to make a suit for next year. I masked from 1947 to 1987, and then in 1988, I was approaching my retirement, and my daughter wanted a big wedding. So I didn't put the money into an Indian suit. I came back and did ten more years, and in 1998, I didn't make a suit. In 1999, I made my fifty-first—it was a pink suit. And 2004 was my fifty-second year. The public is still asking me to come on back one more time. They're missing me. For 2005, I'm making a new suit. I've got it laid out on the kitchen table. That's where I'm working now. It means a lot to carry on this tradition. I want my family to continue with this—my son, my granddaughter Chelsi, and my great-grandson Freddie. It's in my family. It's my life. When Carnival time comes, I got to be there. It's a must."

Tootie Montana posing with his grandson Chantz during Mardi Gras. New Orleans, 1992.

FURTHER READING

Akin, S. Beth. *Voices from the Fields: Children of Migrant Farmworkers Tell Their Stories.* Illus. with photographs by the author. Boston: Little, Brown, 1993.

Belton, Sandra. *From Miss Ida's Porch.* Illus. by Floyd Cooper. New York: Four Winds, 1993.

Bial, Raymond. *Cajun Home.* Illus. with photographs by the author. Boston: Houghton Mifflin, 1998.

Bowman, Paddy, Betty Carter, and Alan Govenar. *Masters of Traditional Arts Education Guide.* With DVD-ROM. Santa Barbara, Calf.: ABC-CLIO, 2002.

Doucet, Sharon Arms. *Fiddle Fever.* New York: Clarion, 2000.

England, Linda. *The Old Cotton Blues.* Illus. by Teresa Flavin. New York: Margaret K. McElderry, 1998.

Garza, Carmen Lomas. *Family Pictures.* Illus. by the author. San Francisco: Children's Book Press, 1990.

Gelber, Carol. *Masks Tell Stories.* Brookfield, Conn.: Millbrook Press, 1993.

Glover, Savion, and Bruce Weber. *Savion! My Life in Tap.* New York: Morrow, 2000.

Govenar, Alan, editor. *Masters of Traditional Arts, Biographical Dictionary.* Volumes 1 and 2. Santa Barbara, Calf.: ABC-CLIO, 2001.

———. *Osceola: Memories of a Sharecropper's Daughter.* Illus. by Shane W. Evans. New York: Hyperion, 2000.

Grimes, Nikki. *Aneesa Lee and the Weaver's Gift.* Illus. by Ashley Bryan. New York: Lothrop, Lee & Shepard, 1999.

Hart, Elva Treviño. *Barefoot Heart: Stories of a Migrant Child.* Tempe, Ariz.: Bilingual Press/Editorial Bilingüe, 1999.

Hill, Laban Carrick. *Harlem Stomp! A Cultural History of the Harlem Renaissance.* Boston: Little, Brown, 2004.

Jiménez, Francisco. *The Circuit: Stories from the Life of a Migrant Child*. Albuquerque: University of New Mexico Press, 1997.

Jones, Bill T., and Susan Kuklin. *Dance*. Illus. with photographs by Susan Kuklin. New York: Hyperion, 1998.

Left Hand Bull, Jacqueline, and Suzanne Haldane. *Lakota Hoop Dancer*. Illus. with photographs by Suzanne Haldane. New York: Dutton, 1999.

Lyons, Mary E. *Catching the Fire: Philip Simmons, Blacksmith*. Illus. with photographs by Mannie Garcia. Boston: Houghton Mifflin, 1997.

———. *Stitching Stars: The Story Quilts of Harriet Powers*. New York: Scribners, 1993.

Major, John S., and Betty J. Belanus. *Caravan to America: Living Arts of the Silk Road*. Chicago: Cricket Books, 2002.

Meyers, Walter Dean. *Blues Journey*. Illus. by Christopher Meyers. New York: Holiday House, 2003.

Orgill, Roxane. *Shout, Sister, Shout!: Ten Girl Singers Who Shaped a Century*. New York: Margaret K. McElderry, 2001.

Raven, Margo Theis. *Circle Unbroken: The Story of a Basket and Its People*. Illus. by E. B. Lewis. New York: Farrar, Straus and Giroux, 2004.

Salisbury, Graham. *Blue Skin of the Sea: A Novel in Stories*. New York: Delacorte, 1992.

Tamar, Erika. *Blues for Silk Garcia*. New York: Crown, 1983.

Yee, Paul. *Tales from Gold Mountain: Stories of the Chinese in the New World*. Illus. by Simon Ng. New York: Macmillan, 1989.

PHOTOGRAPHY CREDITS

Qi Shu Fang: Beijing Opera Performer
Pp. 10, 11, 12, 13, and 14 (right): courtesy of Qi Shu Fang, used by permission.

All other photographs in this chapter: copyright © 2006 by Alan Govenar.

Ralph W. Stanley: Boat Builder
Pp. 16, 19 (bottom), 20, 21 (left), 22 (top left and right), 24 (bottom left and right), and 26: courtesy of Ralph W. Stanley, used by permission.

P. 22 (bottom): Millard Merrick, courtesy of Ralph W. Stanley, used by permission.

All other photographs in this chapter: copyright © 2006 by Peggy McKenna, used by permission.

Eva Castellanoz: *Corona* Maker
All photographs in this chapter: copyright © 2006 by Jan Boles, used by permission.

Dorothy Trumpold: Weaver
P. 49 (left): William Foerstner, courtesy of the Amana Heritage Society, used by permission.

Pp. 50 and 51: William F. Noé, courtesy of the Amana Heritage Society, used by permission.

Pp. 49 (right), 52, and 53 (top right and bottom left): courtesy of Dorothy Trumpold, used by permission.

All other photographs in this chapter: copyright © 2006 by Alan Govenar and Andrew Dean.

Allison "Tootie" Montana: Mardi Gras Indian
Pp. 64, 74, 76, 77, and 80: copyright © 2006 by Alan Govenar.

Pp. 70, 71, and 72: copyright © 2006 by Michael P. Smith, used by permission.

Pp. 65–69, 75, 78, and 81: courtesy of Joyce Montana, used by permission.

ACKNOWLEDGMENTS

In the making of this book, I am grateful, first and foremost, to Qi Shu Fang, Ralph W. Stanley, Eva Castellanoz, Dorothy Trumpold, and Allison "Tootie" Montana for sharing their stories and artistry with me.

The work of photographers Jan Boles, Peggy McKenna, and Andrew Dean complemented my efforts and added visual depth. Jay Brakefield transcribed my interviews and aided me in checking facts and dates. Alan Hatchett assisted me with location photography, lighting, and color correction. Daniel Youd, Cecilia Pang, and Leonora Hsieh were invaluable as Chinese translators. My wife, Kaleta Doolin, daughter, Breea, and son, Alex, energized me in conversations about this book and heightened my appreciation of the ways art and tradition can enhance life day by day.